THE LORD'S WORK
DONE IN THE LORD'S WAY

"I have set the LORD always before me . . ."

Psalm 16:8a

THE LORD'S WORK DONE IN THE LORD'S WAY

K.P. YOHANNAN

BOOKS

a division of Gospel for Asia

www.gfa.org

The Lord's Work Done in the Lord's Way

© 2004 by K.P. Yohannan

All rights reserved.

ISBN: 978-1-59589-017-7

Published by gfa books, a division of Gospel for Asia
1800 Golden Trail Court, Carrollton, TX 75010 USA
phone: (972) 300-7777
fax: (972) 300-7778

Printed in the United States of America

For information about other materials, visit our website:
www.gfa.org.

Dedication

How beautiful it is to see and touch eternal truth lived out before us. We become by imitating.

It was in 1982 that I first met Pastor Chuck Smith. While shaking his hand, my heart whispered, "He really knows the Lord."

These past 22 years of knowing Pastor Chuck, listening to him and watching his life have made the message of this booklet even more real.

Affectionately, I dedicate this booklet to Pastor Chuck Smith, the founder and spiritual father of the Calvary Chapel movement.

Table of Contents

Introduction

I spoke this message to our fellowship on July 30, 2002. It was one of those days especially set apart for prayer and waiting upon the Lord. We began with hours of worship and adoration, during which the Lord became very real to us.

What I share here was the result of a growing burden God gave me during that time, calling us to remember once more that we must *continually* draw near to Him, to hear Him and grow in our love and understanding of Him. To try to do any ministry apart from this is a sad mistake.

Our emphasis—no matter what we do—must always be to know the Lord and His ways. Only then can the work be done in total dependence upon Him. Only then can our work bring Him glory.

May the Lord draw you closer to Himself as you read this.

CHAPTER ONE

God Speaks to Us

I'm looking for one who will wait and watch
For My beckoning hand, My eye—
Who will work in My manner the work I give,
And the work I give not pass by.
And oh the joy that is brought to Me
When one such as this I can find—
A man who will do all My will,
Who is set to study his Master's mind.[1]

Recently in our ministry, there has been a spiritual renewal taking place in the lives of our leaders on the mission field. As a result, these leaders have called for 90 days of continuous chain-prayer, involving thousands of people, to seek the Lord for greater spiritual reality and renewal among those who serve with us.

It all began when some of our senior leaders met for four days of planning and consultation concerning the ministry and what needed to be done. Because the work is growing so fast, we remain with only one thing that is permanent—change. Every two or three years, new systems need to be deployed to handle the increase. People have to be transferred. Strategies must be reworked. It is often out of sheer necessity and urgency that these meetings are called.

Several meetings were scheduled throughout the Indian subcontinent, with the first one taking place in North India with 25 leaders present. As usual, their time started off with the first few hours of the first day's meeting in a time of worship. The room was filled with worship and prayer, but as time went on, the prayers wouldn't stop. They continued on into the evening, and the Lord's presence became very real in that place.

God began to speak through one of the senior leaders in attendance. With a specific word given to him, he spoke what the Lord was saying to the leaders individually. The

Lord knew just what each one was facing in their lives and ministry, and He exhorted them and spoke the exact word needed at that time.

After this, a general message from the Lord was given for everyone in the meeting. The essence of the message was, "You are extremely busy in doing My work and meeting the desperate need of the lost world. You sacrifice and suffer for Me. I am very happy and very pleased with what you are doing for Me. You share My concern, My burden, and I am well pleased. But, at the same time, I am sad because your love for Me is growing thin."

There was no judgment, no condemnation in what God spoke to them. But those words changed the entire agenda for their meeting. Instead of seeking solutions on how to handle the work, their first priority became just to stay in the place of prayer and worship and draw closer to Him.

At the next meeting place, a similar incident happened. God began to speak the exact same message through someone else.

Discerning that this was a serious matter on the heart of God, the leaders called for everyone throughout our work to take time and personally seek the Lord concerning this message.

When I heard what had happened and all that had taken place, I began to think deeply about what the Lord had said during these meetings. It reminded me of what He spoke to the church of Ephesus. He commended them for all the good work they were doing, but then, just like in our leaders meeting, He said, "I am sad also."

> I know your works, your labor, your patience, and that you cannot bear those who are evil. And you have tested those who say they are apostles and are not, and have found them liars; and you have persevered and have patience, and have labored for My name's sake and have not become weary. Nevertheless, I have this against you, that you have left your first love. Remember therefore from where you have fallen; *repent and do the first works* (Revelation 2:2–5, emphasis mine).

In the midst of intense work and ministry, the Lord was saddened. Why? Because their love for Him was fading away.

Nothing about their ministry had changed. The Lord said that He had seen their work, their labor, the patience and endurance that they had in it all. He commended them for their work and the lives they were affecting. But somehow, in it all, their hearts had changed.

My brothers and sisters, we can be in the same danger.

The ministry that was first done unto Him and out of their love for Him now began operating under a different intent. If we are not careful, we can become so consumed with serving the ministry God gave us and forget the Lord Himself.

This is why He cries out to them (paraphrase), "Repent and return to your first love. Then continue with the ministry I have given you. Minister because you love Me. Whatever you do, do it as unto Me."

A Definition

What is doing the Lord's work in the Lord's way? We must properly define it so that we may be able to attain it.

In Matthew 25:40 (KJV), Jesus defines true ministry—doing the Lord's work in His way—in one simple sentence: "Verily I say unto you, Inasmuch as ye have done it unto one of the least of these my brethren, ye have done it unto me."

Christian ministry, by nature, affects and benefits humanity. We serve God by serving people. The ministry that God has called you to is never isolated from the people He has placed in your life. However, there is a balance that must be kept in Christian service. It is not just a balance of external priorities, what is done first and what is done second, but one that runs much deeper and is the well out of which all ministry springs. It is the attitude of the heart.

Doing the Lord's work in His way is living in the awareness that whatever we are doing, whatever ministry the Lord has called us to, forever we maintain the understanding that we do it unto Him. Our service must be rooted in Him, motivated by our love for Him and done with the desire to exalt His name and His name alone.

There will come a time when each of us and the ministry the Lord gave us to do on this earth will be tested by fire (see 1 Corinthians 3:13). Only that ministry which was done in His way will last. It does not matter what it may have looked like on this earth, it does not matter how well-known it may have been or how much fruit it may have seemed to produce. If it was not done as unto Him, it was not done in His way . . . and it will not stand in eternity.

My brothers and sisters, I share this message with you soberly, knowing how easy it is to run about with our own ideas and our own agendas. Everything can look so good and we can seem to be running on the right track. But if our understanding toward ministry has moved from being one of ministry unto Him to getting results, building a name and serving the people, we are dangerously off course.

How All Is Lost

How is it that, even in ministry, we can lose our first love?

It all begins when we neglect to come into His presence and sit at His feet. It is in His presence that we grow in our understanding of Him and His ways, and are equipped to go and carry out the ministry He gave us to do. Our lives take on the atmosphere of living moment by moment waiting, listening for His voice and being sensitive to Him, seeking to do what He desires.

But when we walk away from this, unfortunately it doesn't mean that all ministry screeches to a halt. In fact, the "ministry" can seem to carry on as usual. The need is still there. The people are still there. Yet when we choose to carry on without waiting before Him, we take the first step off of the right road. We may take well-meaning actions to see the ministry continue, but they are independent actions if not born out of His presence.

One of these well-meaning actions, for example, is taking on work that God did not give to us, just because the need is so great, the opportunities seem unlimited, and we are driven by urgency.

I know for our ministry, the need is absolutely huge, mind-boggling. We need to get the Gospel to so many people before they die and are lost for eternity. So it is logical and reasonable to be absolutely committed and fully involved in doing everything we possibly can to reach the lost. But if we do this independent of Him, our love for and intimacy with the Lord begin to fade away and our ministry cannot be pleasing to Him, no matter what kind of fruit it is producing.

As a ministry, we have found that the safest thing we can do is to come into the Lord's presence and draw closer to Him, that we may know His ways and follow His lead. In the beginning of our ministry, we would ask the Lord, "What *more* can we do?" Now it is different. As one of the fastest-growing movements, we are continually challenged and confronted with so many things we could do. So much so that our major concern has become, "Lord, what should we *not* do?"

Another independent action that results in the loss of intimacy and love for the Lord is when we fail to stop and ask Him how He wants His work to be done.

Oftentimes, meeting the current needs becomes more important than *how* ministry is done. It is in response to necessity that we often create new structures, new systems, new leaders and new training, and we just keep being pulled in all kinds of directions. It is easy to be so consumed by the immediate that it eventually becomes the focus.

We can be spending all our time trying to get the track built for the train to run on, trying to organize and facilitate, yet never stopping to consider that maybe the Lord doesn't need all these structures and plans. Maybe He has all kinds of other ways to do this ministry. But we are so consumed with our business mind and structure and logic that we just keep on doing things in our own ways.

Recently I have been increasingly concerned about this, and God's speaking to us has strengthened that concern. I wonder, "Lord, is this the way we should be functioning and serving You?"

We have often seen how God, in His mercy, steps in, like in our leaders meeting, and changes our plans, setting first thing first.

I am so thankful that the Lord had the freedom to come to us in that way even when none of our leaders expected it. It is a relief to know He is with us, watching over the work. It was like spending a day out in hot, humid summer weather and finally getting a good, cool shower. It is refreshing! "Ah yes!" He is with us and He is leading us.

At the same time, I was made aware that we must be careful and concerned about how we proceed in serving the Lord. By no means do I want you to think I am saying we should stop our work and not do what we are doing. That is not how it works. In fact, it seems the more we take the time to wait and hear from the Lord, the more actual work that we do—but rather in His strength, not ours.

This is how the Lord's work is done in His way—by loving Him more than the ministry He gave us to do, by waiting in His presence to hear His voice and by continuing in that sensitivity to Him so that we are always doing His will, in His strength.

CHAPTER TWO

Founded by God

All that brings glory to God and lasts in eternity must have its origin with God, not with ourselves. Ministry is something given to us by God. *Jesus called* the disciples to follow Him; they did not call themselves. *Jesus* called Paul. John the Baptist was a man "sent *from God*" (John 1:6, emphasis mine).

Along with this, there is another principle present all throughout the lives of people mentioned in the Bible. Over and over again we see that *waiting upon God precedes the unfolding of His plan or purpose.*

One example is seen in the life of Isaiah.

It was as he waited in God's presence that he received the call to be a messenger to the children of Israel (see Isaiah 6:1–9).

This is also how it happened with the disciples' ministry after the ascension of Christ. Scripture says, "[Jesus] commanded them not to depart from Jerusalem, but to wait for the Promise of the Father" (Acts 1:4). It was *as they waited* upon God that they received His call for their lives, and *then* they went out proclaiming His resurrection and salvation.

The calling of Saul and Barnabas happened in a similar manner. Acts 13:2–3 tells us, "As they ministered to the Lord and fasted, the Holy Spirit said, 'Now separate to Me Barnabas and Saul for the work to which I have called them.' Then, having fasted and prayed, and laid hands on them, they sent them away."

Notice especially verse two—it was *"as they ministered to the Lord"* that they heard Him and found out His plan.

It was not when they had a committee meeting (although there is nothing wrong with committee meetings). It was not when they met to discuss the tremendous needs (although that is a good thing to do). It did not happen because somebody challenged them and said, "You had better get out there and do something about all those lost people." It was not when they did something that was a nice, wholesome, well-planned and thought-out thing to do. It was as they waited upon the Lord.

Before the world began, God knew Barnabas and Saul would be the ones serving Him in this manner. We see this same principle at work in the life of the prophet Jeremiah. Jeremiah 1:5 says, "Before I formed you in the womb I knew you; before you were born I sanctified you; I ordained you a prophet to the nations."

It is encouraging to know that before the world began, God knew the purpose and plan that He has for each one of us (see Acts 17:26). Whether our human mind and our logic can grasp it or not, it is true. " 'For I know the plans that I have for you,' declares the LORD, 'plans for welfare and not for calamity to give you a future and a hope'" (Jeremiah 29:11, NASB).

However, like Isaiah, Jeremiah, Saul and Barnabas, we only learn of the plans He already has prepared for us as we take the time to come into His presence and hear from Him.

Of Greater Importance

There is also another principle we see all throughout Scripture, one that I am much more concerned about. That is, we must *remain in the attitude of waiting upon the Lord*.

One incident in David's life perfectly illustrates the importance of this.

In 2 Samuel 5:19, we are told, "David inquired of the LORD, saying, 'Shall I go up against the Philistines? Will You deliver them into my hand?' And the LORD said to David, 'Go up, for I will doubtless deliver the Philistines into your hand.' "

And so, after hearing from the Lord, David did what He said, and he was victorious.

A few verses later, David is faced with an almost identical circumstance. Once more the Philistines had stationed themselves in the same valley, and once more, they were waiting to attack Israel.

It would have been natural for David to respond to this battle as he did the one before. After all, the previous plan had been a success, and the enemy and the location were exactly the same. David could have easily said, "Well, it's the same situation so let's just forget about another prayer meeting. We know how to get the job done. Let's go and put these Philistines to flight."

But David didn't do that. Instead, he took the time to *once again seek the Lord*.

Second Samuel 5:23 says, "Therefore David inquired of the LORD, and He said,

'You shall not go up; circle around behind them, and come upon them in front of the mulberry trees.' "

"You shall not go up." Do you see that? God had a different plan this time, and David only learned of it because he lived in the atmosphere of waiting upon God, to hear from Him and obey. By this, his ministry was done in connection with Him and unto Him.

There is the requirement that as we continue in the journey the Lord has us on, we must stop often along the way and find out what He is saying. By doing this, our love for the Lord stays strong, the ministry that began out of that love for Him remains in Him and the work done is accomplished in His way.

There are hundreds of Christian organizations, churches, groups and ministries that began so well. But somewhere along the way, somehow, a lot of them stopped waiting upon the Lord, causing their love for Him to grow cold. As a result, their ministry ended up in the flesh, and once again the Scripture is fulfilled—"Are you so foolish? Having begun by the Spirit, are you now being perfected by the flesh?" (Galatians 3:3, NASB).

God addresses this same issue with His prophets in Isaiah 29:13 (NIV), saying, "These people come near to me with their mouth and honor me with their lips, but their hearts are far from me." They may look real and authentic; they may have started well; their service may appear genuine, but it is not. It cannot be because their hearts are now far from Him.

When we stay in the attitude of continuous dependence upon God, what has begun in the Spirit remains in the Spirit and bears lasting fruit.

Doing the Lord's work in His way is of paramount importance. If we continue the work without His direction, leading and strength, it won't be His work at all. It will be only a hollow shell that might look all right but in reality has no life and bears no lasting fruit.

We must come into His presence and wait upon Him, to hear from Him and know His ways.

CHAPTER THREE

Foundations of Ministry

B ut it's not always easy to wait. If we are honest, we will admit that we are usually restless when we have nothing to do. We need noises and things happening all the time. We want to be kept busy and have something to do at any given moment of the day. Most of us have difficulty just being quiet and still, waiting before the Lord.

Why is it so hard to wait? Oftentimes it can be because our motive in the ministry is wrong.

Why Restless?

In the past, we have had a couple of families on staff with us who left the ministry because they were dissatisfied, feeling as though they were not doing what they considered "real" ministry.

In one particular situation I remember a wife who said, "I came here to serve the Lord, and I have no ministry." This family had two children to take care of, but for her, raising those children in the fear of the Lord, serving her family and being an intercessor for the lost world was not real ministry. She wanted to do something that appeared more significant.

Please understand. It is good to long to serve God in the best way we can. But discontentment, discouragement, frustration and grumbling just because we don't like what the Lord gave us to do is not good. We must be able to discern between truly desiring to please the Lord and our own restlessness and self-seeking.

We must be able to discern what is motivating us in the work of the Lord. A lot of times we can be pulled in many different directions by the needs around us. And we can like it too.

The work of the Lord certainly has its satisfaction for the flesh. There is the crowd of people, the results, the praise, the attention and the "thank-yous"—all of these can really make the flesh feel good. We definitely enjoy the attention, the limelight and the sense of accomplishment and self-worth that come in ministry.

But what we are called to in serving Him must be rooted in pleasing Him and done out of our love for Him—not our own gratification and glory. It must be for His.

Two Kinds of Servants

In Ezekiel 44, we find two groups of servants of God. One group were the Levites who spent their days busy, busy, busy in the outer court of the temple serving the people who came to worship the Lord.

These men were responsible for preparing the sacrifices and getting them ready for offering. Twenty-four hours a day, they were busy in the outer court, where it was full of people and noises. Many people saw the work the Levites were doing; it was a very visible thing. They were dragging the animals in, sacrificing them and putting them on the altar. These men were in great demand by the multitudes, pulled in all different directions, motivated by the screaming needs around them and all that needed to be done.

But there was also another group—the sons of Zadoc. These were men of the inner court. Where they stood, there was stillness. Unlike the outer court, the inner court was silent. Deadly quiet. The only individual there was God. There was no busyness, no service in front of people, no demand but to come into the holy of holies and minister unto the Lord.

Let me ask you—which group are you in? Are you like one of the sons of Zadoc, more concerned with coming into the holy of holies and ministering to the Lord than being busy serving the people? Or do you just keep going, going, going, moved in every direction with the busyness of the ministry? These are serious questions we must ask ourselves.

This reminds me of the story of Martha and Mary in Luke 10:38–42 (NIV).

> As Jesus and his disciples were on their way, he came to a village where a woman named Martha opened her home to him. She had a sister called Mary, who sat at the Lord's feet listening to what he said. But Martha was distracted by all the preparations that had to be made. She came to him and asked, "Lord, don't you care that my sister has left me to do the

work by myself? Tell her to help me!"
"Martha, Martha," the Lord answered,
"you are worried and upset about many
things, but only one thing is needed. Mary
has chosen what is better, and it will not
be taken away from her."

It is clear in this passage, although our
flesh would much rather be in the center of
attention, that the better thing is to be more
concerned with sitting "at the Lord's feet listening," rather than busy with all the ways we
are trying to serve God. It wasn't that Martha's
service was wrong. Not at all. What was
wrong was that "Martha was distracted" from
her first love by all of it. Jesus said Mary "has
chosen what is better"—to leave the busy
place of the outer courts and come into the
inner court and minister to Him.

Purify Our Hearts

But the truth is, we all have the same
problem—wicked hearts. We'd rather be one
of the priests who are busy standing before
the people, active in what is immediately
needed. We want our ministry to look dra-
matic and effective. Our flesh wants to glory
in the praise of men.

Just think about it. If asked to do a job
that is below our educational qualifications

or beneath our dignity, how glad are we? How eager are we to continue if the results are not what we would like?

As humans, we often measure godliness and spirituality by external activities or a certain type of behavior that we see in people. The Pharisees were considered extremely spiritual people by the way they fasted and prayed and put on a humble demeanor.

Yet we know how Jesus spoke of them, identifying them for what they truly were and pronouncing the worst judgment upon them (see Matthew 23:13). Despite how spiritual they looked, they did not know the Father. And without that, all their religious activity meant nothing. The motivation behind all their action was full of self, not love for God. The *motive* is what makes the work spiritual or unspiritual.

We shouldn't worry about how things look, what people might be saying, or whether or not there are the results we thought there would be. Our number-one concern must be to know Him and His ways and to follow His lead.

When we live like this, what happens, whether good or bad in man's sight, whether productive or useless in man's opinion has no bearing. We are not working for human beings. We are doing it because of our love for Him. It is ministry unto Him, and this pleases Him.

May we be reminded of the words of Paul, who facing incredible responsibilities, great need and overwhelming difficulties still said, "None of these things move me" (Acts 20:24). The difficulties and problems, all the blessings and praise, the good and the bad that happened, none of these things changed his course. Issues of personal life or loss did not sway him. All he wanted to do was the ministry the Lord gave him to do. Nothing else and nobody else motivated him.

Please, we need to evaluate what our motive has been in serving the Lord. Are we seeking to meet the need around us, or are we seeking to know and please Him? Are we controlled, motivated and energized by our talents and by opportunities that present themselves? Do needs and others' voices guide our course? Or do we really know, in our innermost being, that we are serving our King? Ask yourself these questions.

Whatever we are doing, whoever we are serving, we must be able to do it all with the heart attitude that we are doing this for no one but our God.

Fruitful Stillness

Please understand. I am not saying that it is better to forsake the work of the ministry to pursue the "deeper life" of just drawing close to God in solitude. There are some who give such great emphasis on this "deeper life," yet so much of the actual work that God has for them goes neglected under the license of "waiting" upon Him. This can often just be a glorified laziness—and there are plenty of verses throughout Scripture that speak of the downfall of the sluggard (see Proverbs 21:25).

If we look at the life of Jesus, we see He was extremely busy—traveling here, walking there, healing her, touching him, speaking from a boat, teaching on a hill. He used His time and opportunities to the maximum.

Yet we also read, over and over again, how He would break away from the crowd and all the activity to be with the Father. His entire ministry, all of the seeming "busy-ness," flowed out of His intimate relationship with the Father.

A.W. Tozer spoke of the need for this today, saying,

> There is no question but that part of our failure today is religious activity that is not preceded by an aloneness—an

inactivity. I mean the art of getting alone
with God and waiting in silence and in
quietness until we are charged, and then,
when we act, our activity really amounts
to something, because we have been prepared for it. . . . We can go to God with
an activity that is "inactive." We go to
God with a heart that isn't acting in the
flesh or in the natural—trying to do something—but going to God and waiting. It
just means that within, our inner spirit is
seeing and hearing and mounting up on
wings, while the outer, physical person
is inactive, and even the mind is to some
degree suspended. . . . There is an inactivity which, paradoxically, is the highest possible activity. There can be a suspension of
the activity of the body as when our Lord
told His disciples to tarry until they were
filled with the Holy Spirit—and they did!
They waited on God.[1]

My brothers and sisters, first thing must
be first. It all comes back to this one priority:
our love for Jesus. No matter how hard we try,
no matter what methods we try, the service
that pleases Him most is the service done out
of love.

CHAPTER FOUR

Purified in His Presence

Why is doing the Lord's work the Lord's way so important? If the job is getting done, doesn't that justify the means?

The answer is no.

Why is it so critical for us to continually take the time to wait upon Him and hear from Him, drawing close and living in His presence? Because when we do not, we are walking in sin.

You see, there are two types of sin that we need to be mindful of. One is the sin of rebellion—we refuse to wait to know what the Master's will is and do what we want to do with an independent, rebellious spirit, void of brokenness and humility.

The second is the sin of presumption. This is where we run ahead with our own plans and in our own understanding, never taking the time to hear what He desires or to find out His ways.

The prevention to each of these sins is found in waiting upon the Lord.

You see, by choosing to come into His presence, we leave aside our agenda and prepare ourselves to submit to His yoke. In His presence we are changed; the independent spirit is substituted for His will and His ways. Our hearts change as a deep transformation takes place within.

Yet it never happens overnight. This process of continually changing and becoming like the Lord only takes place as we take the time to be with Him, to sit at His feet and to gaze upon Him (see 2 Corinthians 3:18).

It is in these times that we are emptied of ourselves and become one with Christ. We experience the joy and victory of knowing that the ministry we have received is from the Lord and for Him (see 1 Corinthians 4:1). It is through this that the Lord can manifest His life and His glory and carry out His purposes through our earthen vessels,

just as Jesus allowed His Father to fulfill His
plan through His life on earth.

Freed for Pure Ministry

Waiting before the Lord and ministering
to Him is so crucial because it deals with the
worst enemy that keeps us from experiencing the fullness of God's life, out of which all
ministry must flow. That enemy is our "self."

As we pull away from the busyness and
all that can seem to clutter our lives and wait
before Him, God removes us from ourselves
and into His pure presence. By this our life
and ministry are made pure, bringing Him
true glory and honor.

As a goldsmith purifies the metal in the
furnace, so our waiting in His presence is the
means by which the Lord purifies our soul.

Hebrews 12:29 tells us that, "Our God is a
consuming fire." As we throw ourselves into
His hands and abandon all that we are—all
of our plans, ambitions, ministry, desires,
everything—the knowledge of the Holy One,
the Consuming Fire, invades every area of
our being, purifying us. The knowledge of the
Lord and the understanding of His ways grad-
ually consume all that is earthly and of self.

Even Job, the man acknowledged by God
as the most godly and righteous person on
earth, still had to go through this fire of

purification. While his friends and wife did not understand the ways of God, he waited before the Lord, crying out, "When He has tried me, I shall come forth as gold" (Job 23:10, NASB).

In her book *Experiencing the Depths of Jesus Christ*, Madame Guyon writes about this change that takes place as we wait upon the Lord, using nature as an example.

> Observe the ocean. The water in the ocean begins to evaporate. Then the vapor begins moving toward the sun. As the vapor leaves the earth, it is full of impurities; however, as it ascends, it becomes more refined and more purified. What did the vapor do? The vapor did nothing. It simply *remained passive*. The purifying took place as the vapor was drawn up into the heavens! There is one difference between your soul and those vapors. Although the vapor can *only* be passive, you have the privilege of cooperating *voluntarily* with the Lord as He draws you inwardly toward Himself. . . . Of course, the closer you are drawn to God, the farther you are removed from the activities of your natural man. The natural man, to be sure, is very opposed to your inward drawing toward God. Nonetheless, there

will come a point when you will finally be
established in [waiting before Him]. From
that point on, it will be natural for you to
live before the Lord![1]

If our outward actions are the result of a
change that has taken place deep within our
hearts—which comes from our intimate fellowship with Him—then what we do has
spiritual value and lasts for eternity.

We don't want to be like the prophets
in Jeremiah's time. They were servants of
God, yet they did not remain in that attitude
of waiting before Him, to hear from Him
and follow His ways rather than their own.
Because of this, their rebellious hearts led
them and many astray. Of them God said,

> "They speak visions from their own minds,
> not from the mouth of the LORD. . . . But
> which of them *has stood in the council of*
> *the LORD to see or to hear his word?* Who has
> listened and heard his word? . . . I
> did not send these prophets, yet they
> have run with their message; I did not
> speak to them, yet they have prophesied.
> *But if they had stood in my council*, they
> would have proclaimed my words to
> my people and would have turned
> them from their evil ways and from their

evil deeds" (Jeremiah 23:16, 18, 21–22, NIV, emphasis mine).

Notice how all this happened because they would not stand before the Lord. They were full of activity—prophesying, preaching, and so on—but it was not done out of standing before Him, ministering to Him or waiting in His presence. Their hearts and ministry were never purified, and the work they did did not flow out of love for Him. Their work was not done in the Lord's way.

The only way we can live a life and ministry pleasing to God is if we come His way—the way of listening, humbling ourselves and continually following. We who began well must be careful to continue on the right path.

We must take the time to wait before Him, looking to Him alone until the whole divine presence comes and fills our soul. This is the only way we are prepared to serve others on behalf of our Lord.

CHAPTER FIVE

No Sweat

When our ministry to the people around us is done as a ministry unto the Lord—doing His work in His way—there will be no striving. There will be no human sweat.

Why?

Because sweat signifies man's effort. The first time sweat is mentioned in the Bible is in Genesis 3:19. Because Adam had eaten from the forbidden tree, God told him, "Cursed is the ground for your sake; in toil you shall eat of it all the days of your life. Both thorns and thistles it shall bring forth for you, and you shall eat the herb of the field. In the sweat of your face you shall eat bread" (Genesis 3:17–19).

Sweat is a result of the curse that sin brought. Because of it, the ground would not yield its fruit without man's effort and sweat.

Scripture also tells us that those who ministered before the Lord in the inner court were not to wear anything made of wool, anything that would cause them to sweat. "And it shall be, whenever they enter the gates of the inner court, that they shall put on linen garments; no wool shall come upon them while they minister within the gates of the inner court . . . They shall not clothe themselves with anything that causes sweat" (Ezekiel 44:17–18).

This is a picture of the kind of service that honors the Lord. Work done out of man's ability, smartness or money can be a horrible sweat. But when you come to the place in your life at which you begin to live and serve in His strength, you understand what it means to bear His yoke, which is easy and light (see Matthew 11:28).

In this way, the assignment He gives you will never destroy you emotionally or physically. It will not tear you apart. Why? Because you are not working in the realm of human talents, resources and strength. You are not

producing it out of your own labor and
sweat. There is no longer any flesh involved.
It is Him—ministry unto Him and empow-
ered by Him.

This brings tremendous freedom and
liberty to laugh and be content and joyful
in whatever comes. It makes no difference
whether you are asked to turn the world
upside-down or just to be a doorkeeper at
the house of God. You simply do the work
that He has given you in the strength that He
supplies as a ministry unto Him.

Forsaking Our Own Ways

Is your life full of suspense, frustration
and discouragement? Are you worried about
the future? Are you anxious and frustrated,
discouraged in the ministry and ready to
quit? Are you one saying, "This ministry stuff
is hard. It's not fair. I just want to do some
ordinary job and have a normal life again"?
Maybe you need to learn from the life of the
prophet Isaiah.

Roy Hession, in his book *"When I Saw
Him . . .": Where Revival Begins*[1] relates Isaiah's
encounter with the Lord. He starts out by
describing him, from the first five chapters
of Isaiah, as being a man full of anger. As a
prophet, he is speaking the words of God,
but you can hear his anger and frustration in

it all. Isaiah is really sweating. He is trying to do what God called him to do, but in his own strength, ability and sweat.

Then in Isaiah 6 something happens.

> I saw the Lord sitting on a throne, high and lifted up, and the train of His robe filled the temple. Above it stood seraphim; each one had six wings: with two he covered his face, with two he covered his feet, and with two he flew. And one cried to another and said: "Holy, holy, holy is the LORD of hosts; the whole earth is full of His glory!" (Isaiah 6:1–3).

Isaiah "saw the Lord." This changed everything. In God's holy presence, he becomes absolutely undone. And not only did he see the Holy One, but listen as he describes in detail the heavenly creatures who cried out, "Holy is the LORD!"

Each seraphim had six wings. Notice how *only two* of the wings were for the work of flying; the other four were *used to veil themselves.*

These were incredibly glorious and beautiful creatures, but the One who sat on the throne was far greater and infinitely more beautiful and awesome. The seraphim didn't want their presence in any way to divert attention from the One who sat on the throne, so they covered themselves with their wings.

Please understand. Isaiah's ministry was preaching! He was a powerful orator—a prophet! But suddenly, as he stood in God's presence with the veiled seraphim, he saw how his work, all his service was just filthy rags because it was done in his own strength. He was striving and sweating doing the ministry.

The same thing can happen to us when we come into His presence. Our strength, abilities and success become of no importance. In His presence, all else becomes shadows. The strength and effort of ourselves are exposed for the frailty they are compared to His.

My brothers and sisters, we must have this type of experience in our ministry. We must *continually* see the Lord. By this our ministry remains focused on the Holy One, and we live in His presence and minister in His strength. Like the seraphim, the majority of our ministry must be not the work, but be ministering to the Lord—in everything seeking to exalt Him, to magnify Him and to bring all the attention and praise to the One on the throne. Like John the Baptist, we must live with the ministry mindset that "He must become greater; I must become less" (John 3:30, NIV).

When God took away Isaiah's unclean-ness, his ministry was transformed and with-out sweat. The same thing happens to us as we continually come before Him. We are taken up with Him and lost in the wonder of His presence. Then our ministry and what we can do no longer matter; it is only Him and seeking to bring Him glory.

My brothers and sisters, this is the way to live! Let us lay down our striving and our sweat and do His work His way. Then there is nothing to get frustrated and worked up about, and our lives bear good fruit that endures for all eternity.

My Personal Experience

How Isaiah was in the first five chapters of the book of Isaiah reminds me of myself in the beginning days of our movement.

The preaching I did in many churches during those days was very judgmental and critical. I used kind words, but inside I was angry all the time. I was frustrated. God had told me to do what I was doing, and I was doing it. I expected people to jump up and down in excitement and join with us to see God's work done, but it wasn't happening that way at all!

Instead, right after I shared about the great need of the lost world, the leaders of these churches would take me out for ice cream, all while having a good time laughing and joking.

It was while driving in North Carolina one day, from one meeting to the next, that I simply could not take it anymore. I was so frustrated and angry, trying in every way I knew how to do the ministry He had called me to and still not seeing the results I expected.

In the midst of this frustration, driving along in a little Chevette, the Lord spoke: "My son, you are so torn up and hurt inside. You are complaining and murmuring like you are against the whole world and the whole world is against you. Just give it up. It's Me. Do only what I ask you to do. That's all that matters. Don't seek for praise. Don't seek for results."

I was on the road for an hour and a half as the Lord spoke to me. When it was over, I was so thrilled and excited to get to the next meeting place because of the incredible freedom that had just entered my life.

I arrived at my meeting and shared, and the Lord touched the hearts of people that night. I couldn't even remember all that I had said. It was nothing I made happen. Many came forward with tears and repentance. I ministered with the awareness that I was there only because He asked me to come. I represented Christ—that was all I knew. I was free, and what I was doing was only for Him. Nothing else mattered. I wasn't looking for results. I wasn't striving any longer. That was one of the significant turning points in my life and in our ministry.

Consecrated Flesh

What are some sure signs that we are ministering in our own strength? When we seek to do the ministry dependent upon our own strength rather than ministering out of the abundance of a life lived in His presence, three things happen.

First, our service becomes self-willed. I see the needs. I make the plans. I have the agendas. I know better. It is ME!

Second, our service is by self-effort. It is my effort. It is my work. It is laborious and produces sweat. It is a pain in the neck.

Third, it is for self-glory. I get disappointed when people don't recognize what I have done. It bothers me when people don't appreciate me or when somebody else gets the appreciation for what I have done. Because my flesh did it, I want something out of it. We are full of our own ways.

Jessie Penn-Lewis was a godly woman greatly used in the Welsh revival. In the book, *Molded by the Cross*, she tells how God dealt with her on this issue.

Then came the climax, when one morning
I awoke and saw before me a hand hold-
ing up in terrible light a handful of filthy
rags, whilst a gentle voice said: "This is the
outcome of all your past service for God."
"But Lord, I have been surrendered and
consecrated to Thee all these years; it was
consecrated work!" "Yes, My child, but
all your service has been CONSECRATED
FLESH; the outcome of your OWN
ENERGY; your OWN PLANS for winning
souls; your OWN DEVOTION. All for Me I
grant you, but yourself, all the same."[2]

Our service can be just flesh that is consecrated to God. But God does not want
flesh consecrated to Him. It is full of wrong
motives, stress, worry and sweat.

For Isaiah, the answer to the problem was
cleansing. He admitted his sin. He said, "Woe
is me, for I am undone! Because I am a man
of unclean lips" (Isaiah 6:5).

The answer is the same for us. No matter
where we are in our journey, when we fail in
our ministry, beginning to carry things out in
our own flesh, we need to come before Him
and repent. He is faithful to cleanse our ministry and purify us for service. For Isaiah there
was the burning coal that the angel brought

to touch his lips. The great ministry Isaiah had happened *after* that incident.

We must have a similar experience, to be cleansed of our own ways so that we may know Him and serve Him in a way that brings Him true honor and praise.

Know Him

Today, as of old, God is searching for those who will do His work in His way— those who will simply seek to know Him and minister out of their love for Him and as unto Him.

In Ezekiel 22:30 God said, "So I sought for a man among them who would make a wall, and stand in the gap before Me on behalf of the land, that I should not destroy it; but I found no one."

Notice the statement, "to stand . . . before Me." God was looking for just one person to simply "stand" before Him, to come into His presence and know Him.

The sad thing is, if you read earlier in that chapter of the book of Ezekiel, you find many people—prophets, priests and princes—involved in active, visible service. But God said (paraphrase), "In all of these I can't find even one who knows My ways. All they want is to know My acts. Just like the children of Israel, they want miracles. They want results. They want things they can see and talk about. But they do not want to know My ways."

How I pray that the Lord would find in us a people who seek the greater thing—sitting at His feet in love and adoration, wanting simply to draw close to our Lord and know Him more. Only when we become people who live in His presence, continually listening for Him, will we be people fully equipped for every good work, able to carry out the ministry He gave us to do.

CHAPTER SIX

Jesus Our Model

J esus is our perfect example of how to do the Lord's work in the Lord's way. In his book *Living As Jesus Lived*, Zac Poonen spoke of this, saying,

> Jesus has not only redeemed us through His death, but also shown us through His life on earth, how God intended man to live. He is not only our Saviour but also our Forerunner (Heb. 6:20). He has given us an example of how to live at all times and in all situations, in perfect obedience to God.

> Jesus did not come to earth as an angel,
> but like us. The Bible says, "He was made
> like His brothers in all things" (Heb.
> 2:17) (His brothers are His disciples—
> Matt. 12:50.) If He had not been made
> like us (His brothers) "in all things," He
> could not have become our Example.[1]

Consider the example He gave us in the Gospel of John. All throughout, we see Jesus saying, "The Son can do nothing of Himself, but what He sees the Father do; for whatever He does, the Son also does in like manner" (John 5:19). "I can of Myself do nothing. As I hear, I judge; and My judgment is righteous, because I do not seek My own will but the will of the Father who sent Me" (John 5:30). "I speak what I have seen with My Father" (John 8:38). "For I have not spoken on My own authority; but the Father who sent Me gave Me a command, what I should say and what I should speak" (John 12:49). "The words that I speak to you I do not speak on My own authority; but the Father who dwells in Me does the works" (John 14:10).

In all these verses, there is a common element—Jesus did nothing and said nothing apart from the Father. Everything Christ did flowed out from His relationship with the Father. Nothing else and no one else, not even Himself, motivated Jesus to do what He did.

Remember when Jesus called His disciples? Nowhere in the Gospels do we read that the Father called the disciples. Jesus went and called the disciples. But when He talked to the Father about them, He said, "I have manifested Your name to the men whom *You have given Me* out of the world. They were Yours, You gave them to Me" (John 17:6, emphasis mine).

Do you see it? The selection of the 12 disciples was not Christ's choice; it was His Father's. Jesus was only doing the Father's will.

The night before Jesus called them He didn't sleep. He "continued all night in prayer to God" (Luke 6:12). All night He stood before His Father waiting for His direction and plan, and "when it was day, He called His disciples to Himself" (Luke 6:13).

He didn't say, "John, Matthew, My Father is calling you." No. He said, "Come, follow me" (Mark 1:17, NIV). And they followed Him.

Another thing we can learn from our Lord as we serve Him, is how He made Himself a servant to the Father. Therefore, it was never external things that motivated Him, but His love for the Father and desire to serve Him and do what He desires.

Jesus never acted merely because He saw a need. He saw the need, was concerned about it, but acted only when His Father told Him to. He waited at least four thousand years in Heaven, while the world lay desperately in need of a Saviour, and then came to earth when His Father sent Him (Jn. 8:42). "When the right time came, the time God decided on, He sent His Son" (Gal. 4:4-Living). . . . And when Jesus came to earth, He did not just go around doing whatever He felt was good. Even though His mind was perfectly pure, yet He never acted on any bright idea that came to mind. No. He made His mind a servant of the Holy Spirit.[2]

Today there are those who seemingly serve the Lord. They do great things and have such apparently great ministries, but the Lord has nothing to do with it.

Jesus spoke of these people in Matthew 7:22–23 (NLT)—"On judgment day many will tell me, 'Lord, Lord, we prophesied in your name and cast out demons in your name and performed many miracles in your name.' But I will reply, 'I never knew you. Go away; the things you did were unauthorized.' "

What can we learn from this?

I know for our movement, there are so

many opportunities and challenges we face. There are students to train, leaders to raise up, missionaries to send out. We need to get the job done. There is tremendous opportunity. The list of things to do is so long, the need urgent and the door wide open.

But we must make sure to follow our Example. "There were many good things that Jesus could have done, that He never did, because they were outside the scope of His Father's will for Him. He was always busy doing the very best things. And those were enough. He had not come to earth to do good things, but to do the will of His Father."[3]

It is wonderful that we move forward as best we can to accomplish whatever job the Lord has called us to do. It is good to be driven and focused and moving full speed ahead. We cannot be slothful. Christ was never lazy or slothful. Neither were His disciples.

But the key question is this: When it is all said and done, can we say like Christ did to His Father, "Father, thank You for the students *You* gave us. Father, thank You for the staff *You* recruited. Thank You for the missionaries *You* sent out and the leaders *You* raised up. It is *You* who gave all these to us, and this work is the work *You* gave us to do."

When we enter into this kind of striveless serving, doing simply what He has given us to do, our lives and ministry change. All the murmuring and complaining that come with trying to make things happen cease. There is no scratching your head, pulling out your hair and going nights without sleep, wondering what is going to happen and how the need will be met.

Why?

Because the work is not dependent on your plans, your meetings or your efforts. You simply allow the Lord to live through you. You enter His rest.

When we serve Him like this, we are able to endure the hardest days and the most painful seasons of life, because it is Christ living in us and He is the One doing the work through us. Our attitude remains one of trust and love, and we are able to say, "Lord, thank You for the privilege You gave me to serve You. I am grateful."

CHAPTER SEVEN

Seven Marks of Service

I want to point out seven things we can be sure of when we do the Lord's work in His way.

What God initiates, He will stand by. Whatever the Lord gave you to do, when you do it His way you can be sure that He will be faithful to you in it until the end. Whether your ministry is administration, giving, serving or showing kindness—if He initiated it, He will stand by it.

Consider Moses as one illustration. He didn't initiate the liberation of the children of Israel. And until the end, God was faithful and took them into the Promised Land. Even though they messed up, God stood by them because He is the One who started it.

But be warned—if someone else initiated it or if you started it, I can assure you, it will be nothing but a burden. If you grab for something, it will become a real problem. But if it begins in Him, He will complete it.

A life that is committed to wait on Him will always be effective, because the ministry originated with Him is fulfilled by Him.

When we do the Lord's work the Lord's way, the fruit remains. Regardless of opposition, enemy attacks or delay, the fruit remains. With Madison Avenue methods, manipulation, tricks, intelligence and money, we can build a lot of things; but they will fade away in time. They will not endure for eternity. Psalm 127:1 says, "Unless the LORD builds the house, they labor in vain who build it. Unless the LORD guards the city, the watchman stays awake in vain."

Our role in ministry is one of a love-slave relationship to our Lord. We will not seek for what makes us happy, more comfortable or better equipped. Our only desire is to glorify Him. Our attitude in ministry will be one of belonging to Him and doing His will. We will say, "Please, Master, I want to be yours and serve You because I love You. I will only listen to You, and I will only seek for Your glory."

In this kind of a relationship, we will have God's authority on us. We will have God's power, provision and protection. When Jesus sent out His disciples in Matthew 28, He shared His authority with them. When He sends us out, He stands by us.

In Acts 27, Paul says to those who were on the ship in the storm with him, "I urge you to take heart, for there will be no loss of life among you, but only of the ship. For there stood by me this night an angel of the God to whom I belong and whom I serve" (Acts 27:22–23).

Paul was not frightened or scared. There was boldness and authority in him. Heaven knew Paul; heaven recognized him because of the authority that was on his life that came from his relationship with Christ.

This kind of ministry will change us into the likeness of Christ. It will lead us into holiness and cause us to love Christ more. It is not the work that will bring about these changes; it is waiting upon the Lord that changes us. When we stand before God, we are transformed.

Second Corinthians 3:18 says, "But we all, with unveiled face, beholding as in a mirror the glory of the Lord, are being transformed into the same image from glory to glory, just as by the Spirit of the Lord." We become like Him as we behold Him. Are you becoming more like Him—the humble One, the broken One, the One who came to serve?

When we do the Lord's work the Lord's way, we remain faithful and committed to what He has called us to. Second Corinthians 4:1–2 says, "Therefore, since we have this ministry, as we have received mercy, we do not lose heart." We don't give up. Not everything is going to go well. There will be hardships, trials and temptations. But the Lord is the One who called us. It is His work, and as we stand before Him, we receive His grace, grace that is sufficient for every season and trial of life.

When our life is over and the work the Lord has given us is completed, our reward will be given to us by the Lord Himself. He is coming back with the reward in His hand. Paul says in 2 Timothy 4:7–8 (NIV), "I have fought the good fight, I have finished the race, I have kept the faith. Now there is in store for me the crown of righteousness, which the Lord, the righteous Judge, will award to me on that day—and not only to me, but also to all who have longed for his appearing."

He is coming to you with the reward for you because you waited before Him, you loved Him, you followed Him—you did the Lord's work in the Lord's way.

If this booklet has been a blessing to you, I would really like to hear from you. You may write to Gospel for Asia, 1800 Golden Trail Court, Carrollton, TX 75010.
Or send an email to kp@gfa.org.

Notes

Chapter 1

[1] Zac Poonen, *God-Centered Praying* (Bangalore, India: Christian Fellowship Centre, 1971), p. 35. Copyright by Zac Poonen, 6 DaCosta Square, Bangalore–560084.

Chapter 3

[1] A.W. Tozer, *The Tozer Pulpit—Vol. 1* (Camp Hill, PA: Christian Publications, 1994), pp. 134–136.

Chapter 4

[1] Madame Guyon, *Experiencing the Depths of Jesus Christ—Vol. 2* (Sargent, GA: Seedsowers, 1975), pp. 53–54.

Chapter 5

[1] Roy Hession, *"When I Saw Him . . .":
Where Revival Begins* (Fort Washington,
PA: CLC, 1975), pp. 17, 21–22.

[2] J.C. Metcalfe, *Molded by the Cross*, ed.
Robert Delancy (Fort Washington, PA:
CLC, 1997), p. 38.

Chapter 6

[1] Zac Poonen, *Living As Jesus Lived*
(Bangalore, India: Christian Fellowship
Centre, 1977), p. 30. Copyright by Zac
Poonen, 6 DaCosta Square, Bangalore–
560084.

[2] *Ibid.*

[3] *Ibid.*

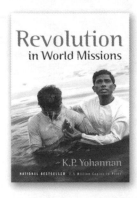

Instill
. . . a passion for the lost.

Impart
. . . fresh zeal for New Testament living.

Stamp
. . . eternity on your eyes.

If you've been blessed by the insight K.P. Yohannan has shared through this booklet, you will want to read *Revolution in World Missions*, his first and most popular book.

When We Have Failed—What Next?

The best *is* yet to come. Do you find that hard to believe? If failure has clouded your vision to see God's redemptive power, this booklet is for you. God's ability to work out His best plan for your life remains. Believe it. (88 pages)

Order online at www.gfa.org
or call 1-800-WIN-ASIA
in Canada 1-888-WIN-ASIA

Booklets by K.P. Yohannan

A Life of Balance
Remember learning how to ride a bike? It was all a matter of balance. The same is true for our lives. Learn how to develop that balance, which will keep your life and ministry healthy and honoring God. (80 pages)

Dependence upon the Lord
Don't build in vain. Learn how to daily depend upon the Lord—whether in the impossible or the possible—and see your life bear lasting fruit. (48 pages)

Journey with Jesus
Take this invitation to walk the roads of life intimately with the Lord Jesus. Stand with the disciples and learn from Jesus' example of love, humility, power and surrender. (56 pages)

Learning to Pray
Whether you realize it or not, your prayers change things. Be hindered no longer as K.P. Yohannan shares how you can grow in your daily prayer life. See for yourself how God still does the impossible through prayer. (64 pages)

Living by Faith, Not by Sight
The promises of God are still true today: *"Anything is possible to him who believes!"* This balanced teaching will remind you of the power of God and encourage you to step out in childlike faith. (56 pages)

Principles in Maintaining a Godly Organization
Remember the "good old days" in your ministry? This booklet provides a biblical basis for maintaining that vibrancy and commitment that accompany any new move of God. (48 pages)

Seeing Him
Do you often live just day-to-day, going through the routine of life? We so easily lose sight of Him who is our everything. Through this booklet, let the Lord Jesus restore your heart and eyes to see Him again. (48 pages)

Stay Encouraged
How are you doing? Discouragement can sneak in quickly and subtly, through even the smallest things. Learn how to stay encouraged in every season of life, no matter what the circumstances may be. (56 pages)

That They All May Be One
In this booklet, K.P. Yohannan opens up his heart and shares from past struggles and real-life examples on how to maintain unity with those in our lives. A must read! (56 pages)

The Beauty of Christ through Brokenness
We were made in the image of Christ that we may reflect all that He is to the hurting world around us. Rise above the things that hinder you from doing this, and see how your life can display His beauty, power and love. (72 pages)

The Lord's Work Done in the Lord's Way
Tired? Burned out? Weary? The Lord's work done in His way will never destroy you. Learn what it means to minister unto Him and keep the holy love for Him burning strong even in the midst of intense ministry. A must-read for every believer! (72 pages)

The Way of True Blessing
What does God value most? Find out in this booklet as K.P. Yohannan reveals truths from the life of Abraham, an ordinary man who became the friend of God. (56 pages)

When We Have Failed—What Next?
The best *is* yet to come. Do you find that hard to believe? If failure has clouded your vision to see God's redemptive power, this booklet is for you. God's ability to work out His best plan for your life remains. Believe it. (88 pages)

Order booklets through:
Gospel for Asia, 1800 Golden Trail Court, Carrollton, TX 75010
Toll free: 1-800-WIN-ASIA
Online: www.gfa.org